D1120044

Be a
Community
Leader

How to Contact an
Elected Official

Leslie Harper

PowerKiDS press.

New York

Published in 2015 by The Rosen Publishing Group, Inc.
29 East 21st Street, New York, NY 10010

First Edition

Editor: Norman D. Graubart
Book Design: Joe Carney
Book Layout: Colleen Bialecki
Photo Research: Katie Stryker

Photo Credits: Cover, p. 24 Blend Images - Hill street studio/Brand X Pictures/Getty Images; p. 4 Photo Courtesy of the Ohio Statehouse Photo Archive; p. 5 Pool/Getty Images; p. 6 overcrew/Shutterstock.com; p. 7 Andrew Burton/Getty Images; p. 9 Nagel Photography/Shutterstock.com; p. 10 sextoacto/Shutterstock.com; p. 11 Gary Conner/Photolibrary/Getty Images; p. 12 Dorling Kindersley/Getty Images; p. 13 Jetta Productions/The Image Bank/Getty Images; p. 14 Juanmonino/iStock/Thinkstock; p. 17 Thomas Barwick /Stone/Getty Images; p. 18 Fuse/Thinkstock; p. 19 massyphoto/Shutterstock.com; p. 20 Eyecandy Images /Thinkstock; p. 21 Joe Ferrer/iStock/Thinkstock; p. 23 Jupiter Images/Stockbyte/Thinkstock; p. 25 Eldad Carin/Shutterstock.com; p. 26 Mandel Ngan/AFP/Getty Images; p. 27 auremar/Shutterstock.com; p. 28 K Woodgyer/Shutterstock.com; p. 29 Jcomp/iStock/Thinkstock; p. 30 Arnold Sachs/Archive Photos /Getty Images.

Library of Congress Cataloging-in-Publication Data

Harper, Leslie.
  How to contact an elected official / by Leslie Harper. — First Edition.
     p. cm. — (Be a community leader)
  Includes index.
  ISBN 978-1-4777-6689-7 (library binding) — ISBN 978-1-4777-6690-3 (pbk.) —
  ISBN 978-1-4777-6691-0 (6-pack)
  1. Political participation—United States—Juvenile literature. 2. Representative government and representation—United States—Juvenile literature. I. Title.
  JK1764.H366 2015
  323'.0420973—dc23
                              2014001408

Manufactured in the United States of America

CPSIA Compliance Information: Batch #WS14PK3: For Further Information contact Rosen Publishing, New York, New York at 1-800-237-9932

Contents

Make Your Voice Heard!

Not all countries are run in the same way. Some are ruled by a monarch, such as a king or queen. Others are ruled by a person or group of people who take control by force. The United States, however, uses a system of government called **democracy**. This means that people choose their leaders by voting in elections. They also have a say in the laws of the country, state, or city either by voting directly for a local law or by choosing leaders who support certain laws.

This statue of Cleisthenes is in the Ohio Statehouse. Cleisthenes lived in ancient Greece and helped bring democracy to Athens.

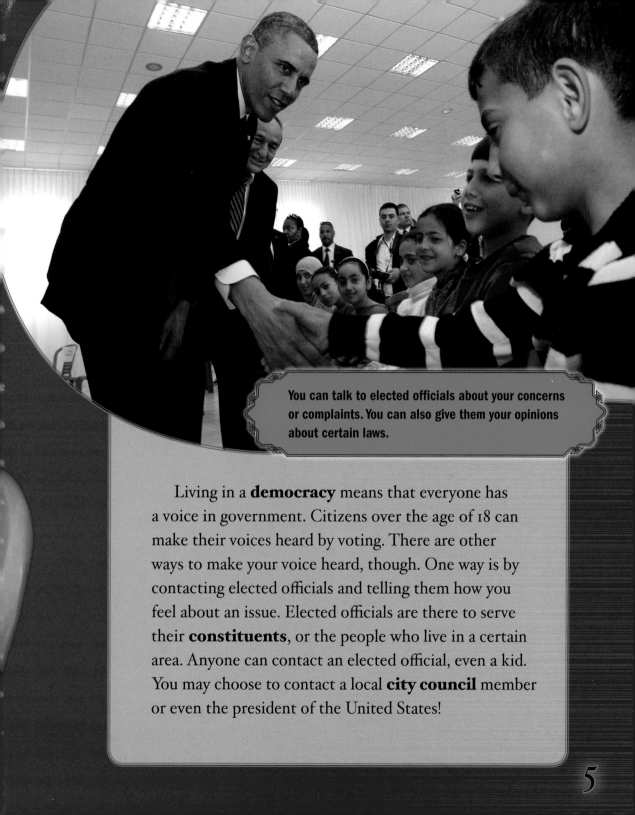

You can talk to elected officials about your concerns or complaints. You can also give them your opinions about certain laws.

Living in a **democracy** means that everyone has a voice in government. Citizens over the age of 18 can make their voices heard by voting. There are other ways to make your voice heard, though. One way is by contacting elected officials and telling them how you feel about an issue. Elected officials are there to serve their **constituents**, or the people who live in a certain area. Anyone can contact an elected official, even a kid. You may choose to contact a local **city council** member or even the president of the United States!

Levels of Government

Everyone who works in the government has a certain job. Some officials are responsible for matters that affect people in a town or a state. Others deal with matters that affect the entire country.

If there is an issue you would like to contact an elected official about, first consider whom the issue affects. If it is something that affects mostly those in your town, start at the city level of government. Towns and cities are run many different ways.

City or county governments usually run fire departments and similar services.

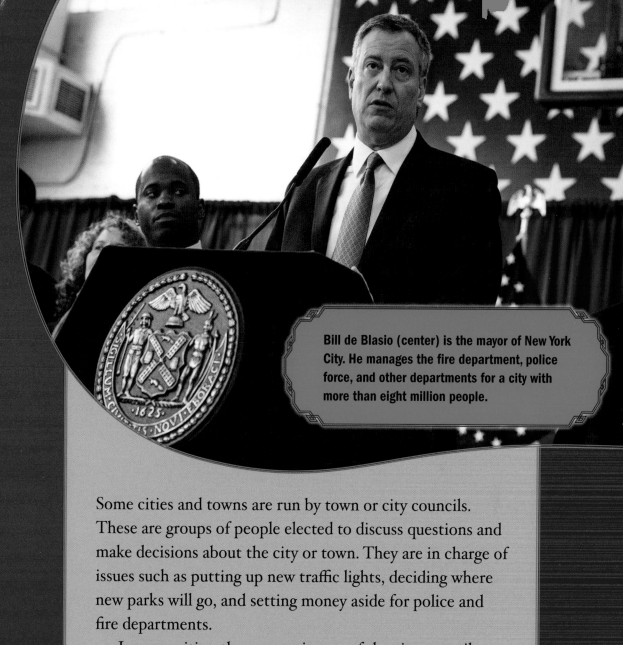

Bill de Blasio (center) is the mayor of New York City. He manages the fire department, police force, and other departments for a city with more than eight million people.

Some cities and towns are run by town or city councils. These are groups of people elected to discuss questions and make decisions about the city or town. They are in charge of issues such as putting up new traffic lights, deciding where new parks will go, and setting money aside for police and fire departments.

In some cities, the **mayor** is part of the city council. In other cities, especially larger cities, the mayor is independent of the city council. He has the power of **veto** over decisions the council makes.

You might want to talk about something that affects everyone in your state. You will then want to contact a state government official. State governments are made up of **legislative** branches, judicial branches, and **executive** branches. The legislative branch is made up of the state senate and the state house of representatives. In some states, this house is called the general assembly or the house of delegates. The state legislature makes laws and approves the state's budget, or plan for how it will spend money. The head of the executive branch is the **governor**. Much like a mayor, the governor has the power to veto laws written by the legislature.

The federal government is set up much like the state governments. The president is the head of the executive branch, and each state sends a certain number of senators and representatives to serve in Congress. If you would like to contact an official about something that affects the entire country, you may want to start with the US senators from your state and the representative who serves your district.

This Michigan congressional chamber has seating for viewers. People are allowed to watch the meetings of state governments.

Exploring an Issue

Is there anything in your city or state that you would like to change? Would you like to see more parks created or to get newer computers in the local public library? When you are thinking about an issue to focus on, you will need to be specific. For example, you may be passionate about raising awareness about local history. What specific action would you like the official to take?

There may be many things about your city or town that you want to change. Focus your effort on one issue at a time.

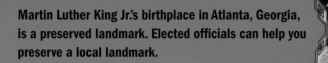

Martin Luther King Jr.'s birthplace in Atlanta, Georgia, is a preserved landmark. Elected officials can help you preserve a local landmark.

Perhaps you learned about some soldiers from your town who fought and died in World War II. Let's say you want there to be a public place where people in your town can honor them and learn about them. Many American towns and cities have memorials to local veterans. If you care about this issue, let an elected official know! Offering specific solutions is always more effective than just pointing out concerns.

501 Auburn

Political Action Tips

When you are thinking about an issue, it is best to focus on specific problems that can be helped by specific solutions. If you tell an elected official that she should do more to honor veterans, she may have a different idea of what that means than you do. However, building a statue in a park is a specific idea that can be put in action.

Getting in Touch

To put your idea in motion, you will want to contact a city government official. This could be your mayor or a member of your city council. To find the best person, ask a parent or librarian to help you find the website for your city government.

This website will likely list the names of the current members of the city council. Once you have a list of names, do some **research**.

Explaining your issue and solution over the phone can be difficult. Ask to meet the official in person.

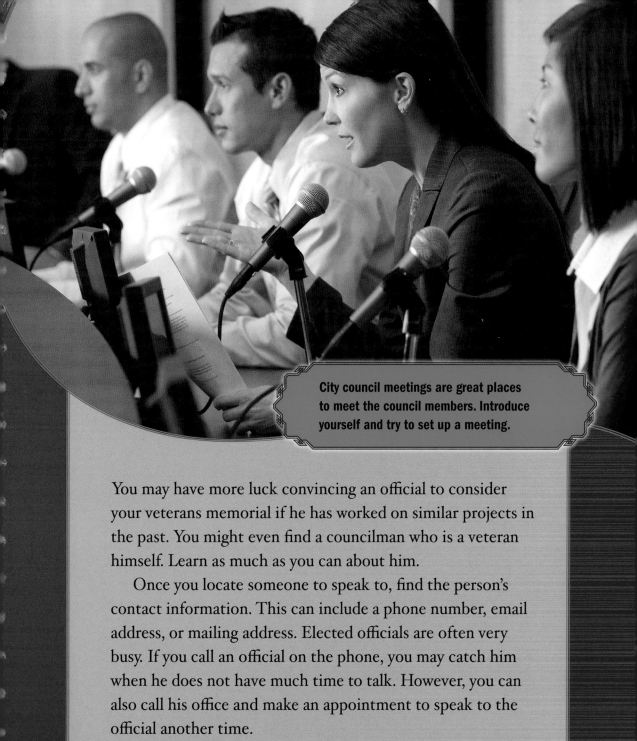

City council meetings are great places to meet the council members. Introduce yourself and try to set up a meeting.

You may have more luck convincing an official to consider your veterans memorial if he has worked on similar projects in the past. You might even find a councilman who is a veteran himself. Learn as much as you can about him.

Once you locate someone to speak to, find the person's contact information. This can include a phone number, email address, or mailing address. Elected officials are often very busy. If you call an official on the phone, you may catch him when he does not have much time to talk. However, you can also call his office and make an appointment to speak to the official another time.

If your issue is a national one, you may want to send a letter to the president. Very often, someone from the president's office will respond.

Attending a town hall meeting, city council meeting, or school board meeting is another way to reach out to your elected officials. Most of these meetings are open to the public. There will often be a certain time during the meeting when the public is allowed to speak.

Sending an elected official a letter through the mail or through email is a great way to get in touch. A well-written letter will clearly explain the problem and offer the solution you would like the official to support. Be sure to keep your letter short and to the point, though. A teacher or librarian can show you some examples of letters that use proper **etiquette**. For example, be sure you address the person by her official title, such as senator or mayor. While some letters and emails can be informal, letters and emails to elected officials should use formal language and proper format.

Political Action Tips

If you decide to write your letter by hand, be sure that your handwriting is neat and easy to read. If an official cannot easily read your letter, she will not be able to understand your ideas and suggestions. If you have trouble writing neatly, use a computer to type your letter instead.

Be Prepared

Elected officials receive a lot of mail and email. Though an issue may be important to them, they do not always have time to respond to each letter they receive from constituents. The first letter that you write may be your best chance to let an official know how you feel. However, there is also a chance that an official will want to talk to you some more about your ideas in person. For this reason, the letter you write should offer enough information to convince an elected official that your idea is worth considering. However, you should also know enough about the issue to talk more about it and answer questions at a meeting.

The first step is to make a list of any questions an official might ask about paying for, designing, and building a memorial. For example, she may ask if the idea will cost the city any money. She may want to know what **benefits** the memorial would provide to the community and whom exactly the memorial would be honoring.

An elected official may want to discuss the issue with his fellow officials. Give him information he'll need to help your cause!

Political Action Tips

You may find it very helpful to present your ideas and plans to your parents or teachers. Then write down any questions they have about the plan. Their questions will likely be much like the questions an elected official would ask you in a face-to-face meeting.

Once you have a list of questions, you can use this list to organize the answers. For example, you might find it helpful to write each question on a separate index card. Then, as you begin your research, you can write the answers you find on different cards. One of your cards might ask how many soldiers from your town served in World War II and were killed in action. Another card might ask whether there are any businesses in your area that could help with this project. Are there any local artists or sign makers who could design your memorial?

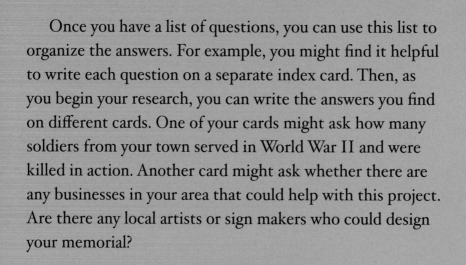

Many word-processing programs can help you make graphic organizers. There are also websites that can help you do this.

Many tourists often choose to visit interesting monuments and memorials when traveling through the United States. A memorial could bring tourists to your town.

Another way to organize your research is in a **graphic organizer**. Graphic organizers are charts, graphs, maps, or other illustrations that organize information. You can start by writing "benefits of memorial" in a circle in the center of a page Then draw lines connecting each benefit, written in its own circle. Some circles could list benefits such as "raise awareness of local history" and "add beauty to the local park."

Research and Resources

You will find research easier when you know where to find the information you are looking for. You school library and local library are great places to start. For research on your idea, ask a librarian to help you find books about World War II and military memorials. You can interview parents, teachers, and other adults to find out if they would support the memorial. You can also use the Internet to find other cities or towns that have recently built memorials or monuments. How have those cities changed since they were built?

Speak to your classmates about your idea. Some of them may give you more ideas to bring to your meeting with the elected official.

You might also want to visit a local historical society. There, you can talk with people who love local history about the memorial you want to bring to your town.

During your research, you should also learn more about how your city council works. Find out where and how often they meet and vote on issues. If you are trying to contact the US representative from your district, find out how often he comes back from Washington, DC, and meets with constituents in the district.

Some areas have historical societies. These organizations work to preserve local history.

Make It Personal

When you contact elected officials about an issue, they will want to know who you are. That does not mean just your name and where you go to school. They will want to know why you care about the issue and why they should help.

You can begin by telling them you live in their district, or the area where those who vote for them live. Elected officials are there to serve the people in their districts. While you may be too young to vote, you can still share your opinion with parents, teachers, and other adults who do vote.

You can also share with the official how you first learned about the issue and how you came to care. You may have had the idea to honor local veterans with a monument during a class field trip to another, similar memorial. Explain to the elected official why both the monument and the larger issue of honoring veterans are important to you and others you know.

Is there a book or website that was helpful to you during your research? Mention it to the elected official during your meeting.

23

Meeting Face-to-Face

If you do get to speak to an elected official over the phone or in person, take advantage of the opportunity to tell her more about your idea. On the day of the meeting, be sure to be on time and prepared. This is an exciting chance to play an important role in your town's government. However, you do not need to be nervous. Talk to the official as you would a teacher or other adult whom you respect. Be polite, but do not be afraid to get your point across and tell the official what actions you would like her to take.

You can bring a friend who also supports your cause to meet the elected official.

Talking Points

- DC Vietnam Memorial

- Important local heroes

- Will raise awareness

Your talking points should all be related to your cause. Do not introduce other issues that might change the direction of your conversation.

Bringing a list of **talking points** may be very helpful to you. This is a list of main ideas you would like to speak about. You do not need to write an entire speech, though. Just include short phrases that will remind you of your main points. For example, you might write "DC Vietnam Memorial" to remind you to mention that the Vietnam Veterans Memorial in Washington, DC, is a major tourist attraction in that city.

The official will likely ask you questions about the issue during your meeting. Answer them as clearly as you can and always have facts to support what you say. If you do not have the answer to one of the official's questions, be honest with her. You might even offer to find the answer and contact her again.

This meeting is also a chance for you to ask questions and learn more about local government and how it works. Ask the official about her job and her responsibilities. Local governments often hold meetings about certain issues to find out what the community thinks. Ask if you may be able to speak about your issue at one of these meetings.

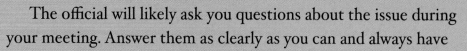

Wisconsin governor Scott Walker is shown here meeting President Obama. Often, elected officials need to work with other officials to get things done.

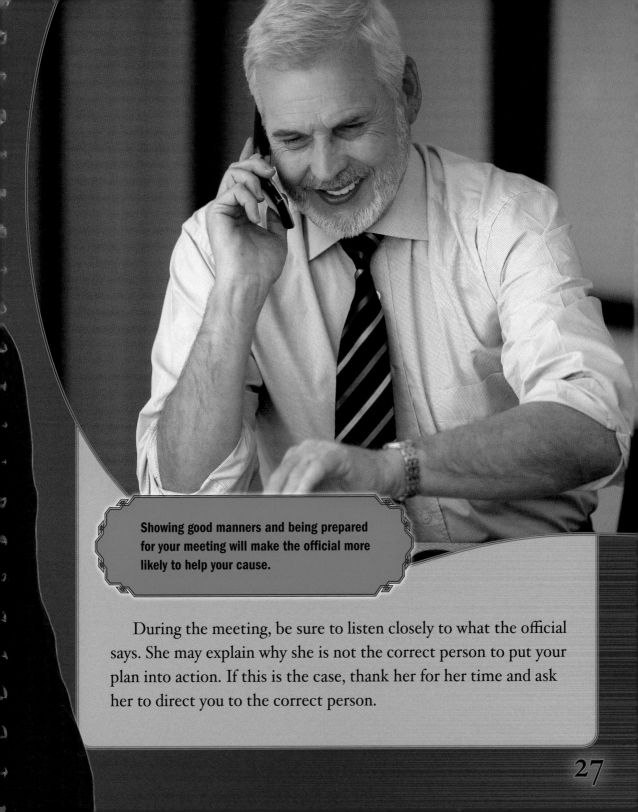

Showing good manners and being prepared for your meeting will make the official more likely to help your cause.

During the meeting, be sure to listen closely to what the official says. She may explain why she is not the correct person to put your plan into action. If this is the case, thank her for her time and ask her to direct you to the correct person.

The Follow-Up

Depending on the issue and when a vote may be held, it could take weeks or even months for you to see any action on your ideas. There are still ways for you to stay involved, though! If your city does begin working on a monument to local veterans, send your elected official a thank-you note. Let her know you appreciate her hard work on the issue. If you are able to build a relationship with an elected official, she may be more likely to listen to your ideas in the future!

Set a follow-up date on your calendar. Use the time between your meeting and follow-up to work out any of the issues that the official raised during your meeting.

6

16

15

14

23

13

22

21

28

20

29

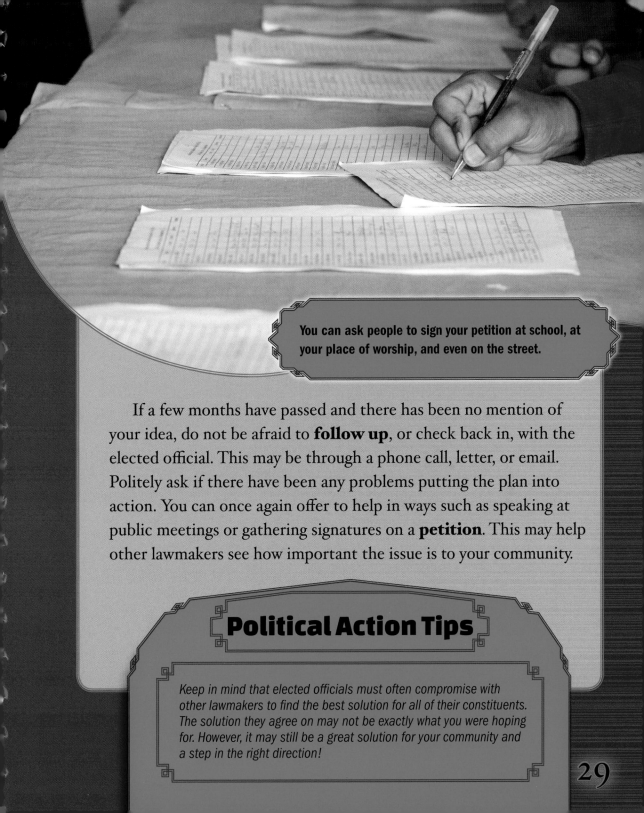

You can ask people to sign your petition at school, at your place of worship, and even on the street.

If a few months have passed and there has been no mention of your idea, do not be afraid to **follow up**, or check back in, with the elected official. This may be through a phone call, letter, or email. Politely ask if there have been any problems putting the plan into action. You can once again offer to help in ways such as speaking at public meetings or gathering signatures on a **petition**. This may help other lawmakers see how important the issue is to your community.

Political Action Tips

Keep in mind that elected officials must often compromise with other lawmakers to find the best solution for all of their constituents. The solution they agree on may not be exactly what you were hoping for. However, it may still be a great solution for your community and a step in the right direction!

Staying Involved

Members of government are elected to serve their constituents. It is their job to respond to your concerns, answer your questions, and do their best to make your community a better place. By contacting your elected officials and sharing your ideas, you can be an important part of that!

While elected officials may have hundreds, thousands, or even millions of constituents, most of those constituents do not make an effort to get in touch and share their opinions and ideas. Contacting your elected officials is a great way to make positive changes in your community. It is also a great way for you to learn about and get involved in local government. Someday you may even choose to run for office. Then, part of your job will be listening to the creative ideas and solutions of kids just like you!

Here, a young Bill Clinton meets President John F. Kennedy. Meeting an elected official might inspire you to run for office someday!

Glossary

benefits (BEH-neh-fits) Helpful or good things.

city council (SIH-tee KOWNT-sul) A group that makes laws for a city.

constituents (kun-STICH-wents) Members of a group who elect another to represent them in a public office.

democracy (dih-MAH-kruh-see) A system of government in which people choose leaders and participate in making laws through an election process.

etiquette (EH-tih-kit) The manners to be observed in social life.

executive (eg-ZEK-yoo-tiv) Referring to the top branch of government, which includes the president.

follow up (FO-loh UP) To contact someone to check in on the progress of a previously discussed topic.

governor (GUH-vun-ur) An official elected as head of a state.

graphic organizer (GRA-fik OR-guh-ny-zer) A chart, graph, or picture that sorts facts and ideas and makes them clear.

legislative (LEH-jis-lay-tiv) Having to do with the branch of government that makes laws and collects taxes.

mayor (MAY-ur) An official elected to be the head of a city or town.

petition (puh-TIH-shun) A formal way to ask for something to be done.

research (rih-SERCH) Careful study.

talking points (TOK-ing POYNTS) Ideas that give support to your argument.

veto (VEE-toh) The power of one branch or department of a government not to authorize laws suggested by another department.

Index

Websites

Due to the changing nature of Internet links, PowerKids Press has developed an online list of websites related to the subject of this book. This site is updated regularly. Please use this link to access the list: www.powerkidslinks.com/beacl/elec/